PSALMS WITH A FRIEND

Psalms

With A Friend

A Devotional Journey Through the Book of Psalms in Ten Weeks

George Coe Love

Dedication

To the congregation of
Hebron Presbyterian Church,
Shepherdsville, Kentucky,
with whom I am privileged to share
the journey of faith.

To Rev. Dr. Robert R. McGruther,
Seminary taught me some things,
Bob taught me how to be a pastor.

And most especially,

To my son,
Cameron Paul Love,
who hung the moon,

to my daughter,
Eliza Kathryn Love,
who added the stars,

and to my best friend, partner,
and lifelong inspiration,
Julie Ann Hager Love.

Table of Contents

Week 1	1	Week 6	71
Day 1	3	Day 26	73
Day 2	7	Day 27	75
Day 3	10	Day 28	78
Day 4	13	Day 29	80
Day 5	16	Day 30	82
Week 2	19	Week 7	85
Day 6	21	Day 31	87
Day 7	24	Day 32	89
Day 8	26	Day 33	91
Day 9	28	Day 34	93
Day 10	30	Day 35	96
Week 3	33	Week 8	99
Day 11	35	Day 36	101
Day 12	37	Day 37	103
Day 13	39	Day 38	106
Day 14	41	Day 39	108
Day 15	43	Day 40	110
Week 4	45	Week 9	113
Day 16	47	Day 41	115
Day 17	50	Day 42	118
Day 18	52	Day 43	120
Day 19	54	Day 44	122
Day 20	56	Day 45	126
Week 5	59	Week 10	129
Day 21	61	Day 46	131
Day 22	63	Day 47	134
Day 23	65	Day 48	137
Day 24	67	Day 49	139
Day 25	69	Day 50	142

Preface

As a pastor and simply as a person who aims to be a Jesus follower, I believe reading the Bible is essential. It's important for us to know what it says and what it does not say and what God is even now, in its pages, saying to us this day. So I encourage folks as much as possible to find time to read the Bible, ideally in a way that becomes habit forming and becomes a regular part of their lives.

The Bible is a treasure, and my passion is to invite you to engage with it and find God in its pages. It's a journey that some find intimidating. Some parts are more accessible than others at first glance. Some parts are simply confusing. Finding ways to engage the text that moves us past any initial feelings that it's too difficult, or too ancient, or too boring are important.

My goal is to create a variety of projects that allow you to move "Through The Bible With A Friend." This initial offering is focused around the book of Psalms. The one hundred and fifty Psalms have been divided up into five daily readings per week to be read over ten weeks. That's five days a week, with two days of grace built in each week. One of the places ambitious reading plans fail is leaving no space for days off. We begin with great intentions, but life comes along and sooner or later we miss a day and we fall behind and our minds tell us we must catch up or quit. Often we quit. Ten weeks of five days a week is a step towards helping us to stay with it. Additionally let me encourage you to be generous with yourself. Five weeks in you may decide you need a week off. Take it. Week six will be waiting for you when you come back.

The picture on the cover is from a summer walk in the woods at Bernheim Forest, a lovely place near our home in Bullitt County Kentucky. My son was home for a visit and he and my wife had walked on ahead, largely because I'm a slow walker. It allowed me to catch this moment, the two of the them walking and talking. I chose this image because it's a good visual representation of what I hope we can do in this book. Walk and talk our way through the book of Psalms. Together.

The Psalms are these beautiful, heartfelt, faith-filled hymns/prayers of faith that people have found deep meaning in for centuries upon centuries. And for the longest time I struggled with them. I divided them into the happy group and the sad group and had difficulty getting deeper than the surface. Then came the pandemic and I decided to try again. This book is the result of that attempt. I finally began to understand the Psalms better and feel the Psalms more. I imagine the feeling is what led to the greater understanding. Whether you have long loved the Psalms or have struggled to dip deeper into this stunning collection of poems I hope our time together will be fruitful.

A brief word on the set up. First, do it however you find works best for you. Second, here's my suggestion. Read the days scripture for yourself. Try to find a place that allows you to focus on your reading. Pause for a moment before you begin and say a prayer asking God to help you to be open to the words of the Psalms you will be reading that day. Then read the text. I'm a note taker and underliner in my Bible reading. If you are comfortable doing that I encourage you to go for it. Another practice might be to pick up a notebook where you can record your thoughts each day on what is going on in your life, what you read in the text and what seemed important to you. After reading and perhaps reacting to the text, check in with me, your companion on this journey. What I've written is my reaction to some portion of what you will have just read. Going at it in this order lets you form your own thoughts and responses to the text before checking in with me to see where my thoughts were led.

I want to express appreciation to Charlie and Betty Hartley, members of the church I pastor (Hebron Presbyterian in Shepherdsville, Kentucky). Charlie helped get this project across the finish line. He was a valuable friend and support, the best combination of encouragement and practical help. Betty helped me avoid errors and mistakes by reading the material with an editorial eye - mistakes that remain are my own.

I also want to thank the entire congregation of Hebron Presbyterian Church. Hebron is a small, country church that is no longer out in the country. Even as the world is ever changing, Hebron continues to be one of the thin places where God's presence feels especially near for many. It has been my privilege to be the pastor of the congregation since August of 2005. I am grateful to them for their love, patience and good humor.

Finally, I want to thank my family - my wife Julie and our now adult children Cameron and Eliza for being the best part of my life. Being husband and being dad are the greatest gifts and I have been exceedingly blessed.

Celebrate Life!

George
Mount Washington, Kentucky,
September 2021

Week One
Psalms 1-17

Day One
Psalms 1, 2, 3, 4

Day Two
Psalms 5, 6, 7, 8

Day Three
Psalms 9, 10

Day Four
Psalms 11, 12, 13, 14

Day Five
Psalms 15, 16, 17

"The Lord looks down
from heaven to humans
to see if anyone is wise,
to see if anyone seeks God...."
-Psalm 14:2

Day 1

Psalms 1, 2, 3, 4

I was supposed to rent an SUV yesterday to use to help our son move his stuff from Chicago to our house on its way to its eventual destination in Durham, North Carolina where he will begin pursuing a Master's in Public Policy at Duke this month. That is supposed to happen tomorrow. That same SUV will then on Wednesday be filled with the belongings of my daughter, who is presently at our house after graduating college, in order to move her, also, to Durham, North Carolina by the end of this week, where she will be studying at Duke Divinity School, working on a Master's of Divinity.

That is a lot of Duke for a Kentucky basketball fan, but it's a good school...and I digress. In order to assist in moving all that stuff I was supposed to have rented an SUV to pick up Tuesday morning. I can do it today, but if I had done it yesterday I wouldn't have to - that's my first thought as I wake up this morning.

Which gets to a problem with my devotional practices. The early morning is my sweet spot for my devotional time. I like to wake up when it's dark outside and still throughout the house.

When the world hasn't gotten started yet, is my time to read scripture and the reflections of others on scripture or on the life of faith. My idea is that I can get to that stuff before the sun comes up; everything else starts to move, and the concerns of the day begin to wake and stir themselves.

This would work great if the first thing in my head before I turn on a light or make a move to climb the stairs to my preferred morning devotional spot is not renting an SUV and all the subsequent moving that needs to be done.

Psalm 1 says that the "truly happy person...loves the Lord's Instruction, and they recite God's Instruction day and night." I want to be a happy person, and I want to follow God's instruction and do that reciting day and night thing, but my mind is a jumble of SUVs needing to be rented and a whole host of other things of varying importance that all want to push to the front of the line.

It's likely you have your own version of this dilemma – as much as we may want to quiet our minds, there is often a lot that wants attention and it wants attention now.

So today we begin our journey through the Psalms. We make our effort to stand up to the demands of the day and find space to immerse ourselves in the ancient poetry of scripture.

I plan to try to do my initial reading of the Psalms for the day in the early morning - hopefully, revisiting them at least once more at some point during the day for a second hearing. I hope you will find a time and a place that you can dedicate to this purpose and that it will become a treasured place in these next ten weeks.

One of the pitfalls of daily devotionals and going through anything in a set amount of time is what happens if we miss a day. Or two. Do we double up another day? Do we inevitably fall farther behind? Do we reach the point where we decide to set it aside and try again another time? To help mitigate that outcome our schedule is limited to readings for Monday through Friday. This leaves weekends free to pick up a day or two that we may have missed during the week or to return to a reading that was particularly impactful during the week. The intent is to provide space for grace and help us to all arrive at Psalm 150 together ten weeks from now.

I think one thing we find will be this: the Psalmist knows what it is to need to rent an SUV. Okay, not exactly that, but the Psalms are full of the language of a desire for God and a recognition of the myriad distractions of life.

And the reality that it is often in what seems to be the myriad distractions that life is actually lived and God is discovered. I've been looking forward to this project and to what we'll find along the way.

I hope that in addition to reading along, you'll make your own notes as we share the journey - both on what we find in the Psalms and how what we find interacts with the immediate circumstances of our lives today. Let's get started - and good luck with all that you need to accomplish this week.

Prayer

Lord, help us to bring all of ourselves to all that you have for us as we journey through the Psalms. Amen.

Our Family, Ready To Head For Durham

Day 2

Psalms 5, 6, 7, 8

I remember watching Roadrunner and Wile E. Coyote cartoons when I was a kid. A lot. I loved the Roadrunner - so much personality, so inventive, always finding a way to walk away from situations with the upper hand. I usually wound up feeling a little remorse for Wile E. though as well. It wasn't that I wanted his nefarious actions to be rewarded. I didn't want harm to come to the Roadrunner, but I felt bad that the elaborate plans that the Coyote spent so much time on were in every instance doomed to complete failure and in fact would often come back in ways he hadn't imagined to harm himself. He took a lot of long, hard, falls that were pretty devastating, even for a cartoon character.

I've long had the same sort of sympathy for the "enemies" who show up in the Psalms. The Psalmist is regularly on about enemies who are really bad folks, almost cartoonishly so, and about the ways God should and will make them suffer for their evil.

In Psalm 7, for instance, the enemy is "the wicked" who "hatch evil, conceive trouble, give birth to lies! They make a pit, dig it all out and then fall right into the hole that they've made." (7:14).

See. Wile E. Coyote, painting a tunnel on the side of a rock mountain and then running headlong into it.

Often times the enemy passages came off as self-righteous to me. Should we take the word of the Psalmist, believing the writer is innocent and the enemies are really as uniformly bad as we are being led to believe? It's like forever hearing one side of a dispute.

One of the ways I began to make progress with passages like this is to imagine the whole thing as an internal drama. Surely there are people who I have issues with at times and perhaps some of the time I am right and they are wrong, but I know myself well enough to know that a good bit of the time I am as much or more to blame for any issues I have with folks I imagine to be adversaries. But what if the whole thing is about the constant internal conversation I have with myself?

Think of the Apostle Paul's idea that he sees the good he wants to do and finds himself doing the exact opposite as a regular practice. What if I'm the Coyote, rigging weights in trees with my actions which will inevitably fall on my head because it was foolish to ever put weights in trees in the first place? What if I am the person who wants very much to be righteous and also the person who thwarts that desire on far too many occasions?

Surely the Psalms are not intended to be taken always as an internal psychological drama and yet there is truth in the mixed nature I find within myself as I careen back and forth between one whose trouble will come back on his own head and one who has the wisdom to thank the Lord for his righteousness, singing praises to God's name. I can be both of those people and recognizing that in the Psalms the Psalmist has guided me to new meaning in these poems of the wicked and the just.

Prayer

Help me to paint fewer tunnels on rock mountains, so that not running into them I can more often be healthy and sing your praises. Amen.

Day 3

Psalms 9, 10

Yesterday didn't really count as a troubling time. It was just long. We spent the morning loading my daughter's belongings into a couple of vehicles (that rental SUV turned into a Dodge Caravan), and then drove for what felt like one hundred and seventeen hours from Mount Washington to Durham, North Carolina (actually only about ten hours). It rained a couple of times, but the drive was mostly pretty. So, a long day, but not a troubling one.

As the drive was reaching its final third, somewhere around Wytheville, Virginia, the GPS on my phone spoke. It told me we were going off the interstate and that it would save us twenty-three minutes. I thought we were going to see some interesting backroad and eagerly bought in to the proposal. The backroad was pretty much the service road that ran exactly alongside the interstate. It kept me over there for a few miles and eventually put me back on the very same interstate. At first I had no idea why we were doing this. All I knew was the interstate was right over there, in plain view, so I wasn't sure why we chose this decidedly non-scenic route. Then it became obvious.

Turns out the GPS knew that there was a line of traffic that stretched on for a very long way. I was moving and they were not. When I was guided back onto the interstate the traffic was beginning to move again. I don't know the exact amount of time we saved, but I'm guessing twenty-three minutes would have been about right – at least. Not twenty-three minutes faster, but instead, twenty-three minutes not lost to sitting in slow to non-moving traffic.

It made me think of Psalm 10:1 which I had read earlier in the day.

> "Why do you stand so far away, Lord
> hiding yourself in troubling times?"

Often, when I imagine that God seems far away, sometimes in times that really are troubling, I think it has something to do with my perspective. It's not so much that God has moved as that God is not where I imagine God should be. God may be at work in my life and I may be looking over at the interstate (where I think my life should be) and wondering why God is over there. That can seem a pretty random place to be in life when you are pretty sure the place to be is the big, impressive highway where all the people are who are really going somewhere. It can seem a frustrating place to be when I am hurting and I'm sure the great reason I'm hurting is because I am on Nye Road and that God has forgotten about me and is busy with all the folks driving carefree down the interstate.

Then sometimes I have a moment when the pieces fall into place before my eyes. The reality is that God is actually right there in the van with me on Nye Road driving past the Waffle House. God does not leave us. God does not stand far away. Good times or troubling times. God is with us.

Prayer

Help me to trust even when it is hard. Amen.

Day 4

Psalms 11, 12, 13, 14

Fake news. Fact checks. Public figures statements are graded by the *Washington Post* in terms of how many Pinocchios they earn as regards their relationship with the truth. One way of living in this world of free-wheeling truthiness is to go all in and try to figure out how to make it work for us. What version of the truth best suits me today? Do I tell the truth that may damage me a bit or cast me in an unattractive light (which might also be known as the unvarnished truth) or do I tell the truth I like and in which I like how I come across better (which might also be known as not the truth)?

The group of Psalms for today all brush up against the ultimate reason why truth matters.

"But the Lord is in his holy temple.

The Lord! His throne is in heaven.

His eyes see -

his vision examines all of humanity." (11:4)

While Psalm 11 is reminding us that God's eyes are on all that goes on, Psalm 12 is about how much everyone the psalmist sees seems to be in love with lying.

"Everyone tells lies to everyone else;

 they talk with slick speech

 and divided hearts." (12:2)

This leads to boasting and misplaced confidence in the power of words to gloss over reality, as people brag...

"We're unbeatable

 with our tongues!

 Who could get the best of us

 with lips like ours?" (12:4)

Psalm 14 begins with the declaration...

"Fools say in their hearts,

 There is no God." (14:1)

but answers that foolishness with the truth that,

"The Lord looks down

 from heaven to humans

 to see if anyone is wise,

 to see if anyone seeks God...."(14:2)

Truth matters. Accurately viewing and representing reality is important. It's not a matter of shaping reality in such a way that we can convince others to see truth where there is no truth even if such a thing is possible for a time.

What these Psalms remind us is that God is not taken in by our embellishment and careful packaging of what is happening in our lives and in the world. God sees us as we are and reality as it is.

Prayer

Keep me ever mindful that I'm not getting away with anything. Amen.

Day 5

Psalms 15, 16, 17

Psalm 15 is lovely and discouraging depending on how it is read.

"Who can live in your tent, Lord?
 Who can dwell
  on your holy mountain?"

The answer looks like it might be no one. It requires someone who...

"lives free of blame,
  does what is right,
  and speaks the truth sincerely;
  who does no damage with their talk,
  does no harm to a friend,
  doesn't insult a neighbor..."

I am quite sure I have been on the wrong side of all that stuff, and likely will fall short – stumble, to borrow the psalmist's word –again in the future. So what do we do with this?

Robert Alter is a professor of Hebrew and Comparative Literature who has produced a wonderful translation of the Psalms,[1] as helpful for its explanations of his choices in translation as it is for the translation itself. He has become my most regular companion in these early days of reading through the Psalms when I'm looking for another viewpoint or insight into a passage. He points to a characteristic of Hebrew poetry that is subtly on display in this passage.

Hebrew poetry will often repeat an idea one or more times in a parallel manner, sometimes simply restating the idea with different words, sometimes intensifying or advancing the idea. Alter points to verse one here as an example of this subtle intensification of an idea. The first line in Alter's translation reads like this...

"Lord, who will sojourn in your tent,
  who will dwell on Your holy mountain?"

The choice of sojourn to go with tent, implies a remembrance of the days in the wilderness with the tabernacle, temporary housing in temporary home. The word dwell combined with holy mountain is reference to taking up residence on Mount Zion, God's more permanent home in the fixed structure of the temple.

---

[1] Alter, Robert. *The Book of Psalms: A Translation With Commentary*, W. W. Norton & Company, 2007, 48.

The progression suggested here is the same sort of progression that is desired in my personal behavior and moral choices. Will I get everything right all the time because I love God? I will not. But will I aspire to follow God more faithfully, lean into God's grace more daily, keep marching to Zion? That's my hope and I believe one that God shares.

Prayer

Keep me moving from tents of right actions towards more permanent structures built on an ever growing desire to respond to your love and live out your grace. Amen.

Week Two

Psalms 18-31

Day 6
Psalm 18

Day 7
Psalms 19, 20, 21

Day 8
Psalms 22, 23, 24

Day 9
Psalms 25, 26, 27

Day 10
Psalms 28, 29, 30, 31

"Weeping may stay all night,
but by morning, joy!"
-Psalm 30:5

Day 6

Psalm 18

An interesting bit about Psalm 18 – it is virtually a copy of a thanksgiving song attributed to David that appears in 1 Samuel 22. Robert Alter suggests that the 1 Samuel version is an earlier rendition as the few places where there are differences indicate an editor perhaps working for greater clarity in Psalm 18.

There is a dynamic, nearly euphoric feel to this Psalm as it opens. This is born of the deep level of distress that the psalmist, named here as David, has experienced.

"Death's cords were wrapped around me;
   rivers of wickedness terrified me.
 The cords of the grave surrounded me;
  death's traps held me tight." (18:4-5)

God has heard David's cries and delivered him. The sense of elation is real.

"From on high God reached down
  and grabbed me;
 he took me out of all that water.
 God saved me from my powerful enemy,
  saved me from my foes,

who were too much for me." (18:16-17)

It is miserable to be in that place where no answers seem to be available. Where it is easy to come up with one bad scenario after another, but the possibility of a good resolution is beyond imagination.

God has a way of standing with us in those difficult and challenging times and leading us to a place we could not have arrived on our own. We often describe this by saying, "I don't know how I could have gotten through this without God."

It is a good practice, perhaps, for us in such moments to write our own Psalms, to compose our own songs of praise. It is useful for us to follow the example of David and not only feel the joy of God's deliverance, but also speak of it in a public way.

If we have experienced God's hand guiding us in circumstances where we believe we otherwise would have been lost, imagine the feeling of desolation one might feel who does not look to lean on God in such a moment.

Our sharing our faith is not meant to be a strong arming of someone to think and believe as we do, but a pointing to what God can mean to any of us when we are in those difficult cords of death and distress that David so vividly described.

Prayer

I love you Lord, my strength, my solid rock, my rescuer. I take refuge in you, my shield, my salvation and my place of safety. Amen. (Adapted from Psalms 18:1-2.)

Day 7

Psalms 19, 20, 21

I end almost every sermon with the words, "Thanks be to God. Amen." It's my shorthand version of the final verse of Psalm 19:

"Let the words of my mouth

and the meditations of my heart

be pleasing to you,

Lord, my rock and my redeemer." (19:14)

I can't know the fullness of what the psalmist had in mind, but for me it's an expression of gratitude and hope. Gratitude for the opportunity to speak of the good news of God's love each time that opportunity presents itself. Hope that through God's Spirit at work in the words they become something more than what they would be if they were simply my words and thoughts. I don't think one needs to be a preacher to put this sort of capstone on an interaction with another person, on a meeting, on the contents of one's day.

It's all a gift. There is a t-shirt by the company *Life Is Good* that reads,

Life is not easy.

Life is not perfect.

LIFE IS GOOD.

That's a t-shirt full of truth. The complexities of life are never going to be easily managed. We aren't going to make it through the day without some mistakes, missteps, and wishes for do-overs. But life is always going to be a gift. Life is good.

So what will we do with it? Our goal is to do our best to point to the reality that God is undeniably with us everywhere, every day at all times.

"Heaven is declaring God's glory;
   the sky is proclaiming his handiwork.
  One day gushes the news to the next,
   and one night informs another
   what needs to be known." (19:1-2)

As we live imperfectly in our imperfect world we point beyond the imperfections to the perfect glory of God. Each day is an opportunity to recognize, rejoice in, and proclaim the presence of holiness. Thanks be to God. Amen.

Prayer

As one day gushes to the next, so let the words of my mouth and the meditations of my heart be pleasing to you and gush forth your praise, Lord, my rock and my redeemer. Amen.

Day 8

Psalms 22, 23, 24

Psalm 23 resides in a special kit that also includes the Lord's Prayer, the hymn Amazing Grace, and perhaps in some instances, the Apostles Creed. It is a part of these very familiar groupings of words that speak well beyond their words to the experience of faith.

I have carried them with me into so many difficult circumstances. When visiting with someone who seems to be non-responsive, these touchstones of the faith speak to deep places within people's beings.

Sometimes the person is alone and after giving a report of how things are going at church - the Yard Sale is a real success, a family is back from vacation and had a great time, the prayer group met and you were prayed for by name - I will ask if I can read a couple passages from scripture. Invariably the 23rd Psalm bats lead off. And an amazing amount of the time there seems to be some response or recognition as the familiar words are read aloud.

Recognition that might best be described as the same sort of recognition one might show if a caring person placed a blanket on you when the room was a little too cold. Your visage might show a bit of gratitude, you might relax a bit in the comfort of the pleasant warmth.

There are promises here of God's provision that become so internalized over the years that simply hearing the words, "The Lord is my shepherd..." takes us to a better, more secure place where we are reminded that, whatever the present troubles, our loving God stands with us and cares for us.

Prayer

Dwell with me my whole life long, in times of joy and times of sorrow, in days that seem to stretch on forever and in days when twilight sets in. I long to know you as my shepherd, feast at your table and know you all the days of my life. Amen.

Day 9

Psalms 25, 26, 27

As a Christian my professed belief is that God came to earth in the person of Jesus Christ. Jesus then lived, died and rose again, forever defeating the power of death and making possible life abundant and everlasting. Naturally, as a result of these beliefs I am never fearful.

Ha!

I'm all sorts of fearful. At every step along the way in my fifty-plus years I can name something that I was, or presently am, fearful about. Unimportant things, important things, things that were real and things that I imagined.

Living in these days, just hearing the word "pandemic" or "Coronavirus" or "COVID-19" is enough to at least get fear within me awake and alert. And that's just the most obvious example I could come up with, there are other fears that we are living with, nurturing and feeding regularly in our culture that will not be denied.

"The Lord is my light and my salvation.

Should I fear anyone?

The Lord is a fortress

 protecting my life.

Should I be frightened of anything?" (27:1)

Should I be frightened of anything? I think the answer is no, and yet, here we are. And we are in good company, the person asking the question is fearful as well just moments later within the same poem.

"Don't neglect me." (v.9)

"Don't leave me all alone." (v.9)

"Don't give me over to the desires of my enemies...." (v.11)

Fear will creep in. It will plant and nurture seeds, hoping to grow something large and monstrous. Faith reminds us that when fear asserts itself, God stands with us. While fear continues to be a part of my journey, my faith gives me the best tool for meeting my fear and trusting that my light, salvation and fortress - my God - is ever with me.

Prayer

My list of things I have feared, am fearing and will fear in the future is long. When I am covered over in my fears, lift me up so that my head is higher than the fears that surround me and let my heart rest in you. Amen.

Day 10

Psalms 28, 29, 30, 31

Have you ever gone to bed in the evening with an intractable problem working in your mind? Even as light turns to darkness, day turns to night, so it can feel like the problem becomes increasingly difficult. Night closes in and there seems to be no answer to the problem. It will not relent. Something happens though. We may lie in bed thinking we will never go to sleep and that this problem will remain with us forever. But then, sleep comes. We wake up in the morning and just as the light announces a new day full of possibilities, there are times when the problem that seemed so ferocious in the cover of dark, loses its teeth in the light of morning's glory.

"Weeping may stay all night, but by morning, joy!" (30:5)

The psalmist goes on in Psalm 30 to thank God for changing "mourning into dancing." (30:11). In the next Psalm there is a similar transformation:

"You didn't hand me over to the enemy,

but set my feet in wide-open spaces." (31:8)

It can feel like that is what is at stake. The night falls, options disappear, and it feels as though God may be tip-toeing away along with every good possibility. Morning comes and it turns out that not only is God still present, but things are not as bleak as they seemed in the darkness. We are not in the tight, hopeless spot we thought we were - we are in fact placed by God in wide-open spaces. Sometimes nothing changes and everything changes. Night gives way to morning, weeping to joy, mourning to dancing. God blesses us with a renewed sense of opportunity in the wide-open spaces of a new day.

Prayer

When weeping stays all night, keep me hopeful for joy in the morning. Amen.

Week Three

Psalms 32-44

Day 11
Psalms 32, 33, 34

Day 12
Psalms 35, 36

Day 13
Psalms 37, 38

Day 14
Psalms 39, 40, 41

Day 15
Psalms 42, 43, 44

"Trust the Lord and do good;
live in the land and farm faithfulness."
-Psalm 37:2

Day 11

Psalms 32, 33, 34

I do not know where anything is in Durham, North Carolina. I was here for a brief time with Eliza when we moved her in, and now, about a week later, am back with Cameron, moving him into his apartment. Yesterday included trips to a grocery store and a trip to Target. We found the grocery store by searching on the internet and we found the Target by letting Eliza drive (she's been here a week and she likes Target so I'm not sure if she was using GPS or just knows where it is already).

My point is, in this new and unfamiliar place we could just go out and start driving and hope we find something that is close to what we are looking for - which actually is a good way to learn your way around a new place if you have the time to do that - or we could intentionally seek out the specific places we would like to find using the technological resources at our disposal.

"I sought the Lord
    and he answered me." (34:4)

There are times when God is in our midst - I think all the time actually God is in our midst - and we don't realize that presence. There are probably many ways that can happen, but I think sometimes it's just that we are looking for other things.

God does not always demand to be front and center in our lives. God gives us spaces to make choices and decide what will be the priority of the day, the month, or the year.

Our choices are not always great. Sometimes it's simply selfishness, sometimes we experience the world as the ocean rolling in at high tide and we find ourselves absorbed by the deluge. In this instance the Psalm reminds us that one way to heighten our awareness of God, to hear God speaking to us, is to seek God out with intention and purpose.

The tools are familiar, prayer, scripture reading, worship, key moments of orienting ourselves to God in the morning as we begin the day and in the evening as we finish it out. God is not lost, but it is a great practice to set our heart on seeking God to help insure that we won't be either.

Prayer

Help me to seek you and listen for your answer, to turn my face to you and shine in your glory. Amen.

Day 12

Psalms 35, 36

I'm good at thinking how I will get to things I need to do, want to do, would enjoy, once things I don't want to do that are unpleasant are complete and all of the obstacles of life are out of the way. The name for that is not being practical or realistic. The name for that is finding reasons to procrastinate.

Psalm 36 feels familiar in that way to me. The psalmist is really wanting bad things for the opposition. If they are they chased, the psalmist wants to chase, if they are the dust about to be blown away, guess who wants to be the wind. God is implored to gather up gear for battle and join in the fray against the adversaries. At the end there is a promise of praise if the right folks get what they have coming.

"Let those who exalt themselves over me

be dressed up in shame and dishonor.

But let those who want things

to be set right for me

shout for joy and celebrate!" (35:26-27)

Concluding the poem with:

"Then my tongue will talk

all about your righteousness; it will talk

all about your praise all day long." (v.28)

I recognize this pattern as similar to my own. Once we have things as we want them we will be the people we ought to be in the first place. It's human and I'll do it again, and I'll have the psalmist as a biblical companion in my error, but it's a good reminder to praise God in all things, beginning now, not sometime off in the future. God is worthy of praise now.

Prayer

Keep me from procrastinating on the things that would be my best actions. Perfect is not walking through that door today - remind me of that and call me to love you now. Amen.

Day 13

Psalms 37, 38

The Common English Bible offers a quirky translation of Psalm 37:2 - I couldn't find anyone else who went this direction.

"Trust the Lord and do good;

live in the land and farm faithfulness."

The unique bit is the suggestion to "farm faithfulness." I'll use this as another exhibit in my argument for keeping at least a couple of translations on hand. This is easily done by actually having a few different versions of the Bible available or, in a wonderful gift of technology, using a site like biblegateway.com that lets you enter any passage and then view it in a wide variety of translations with a few simple clicks. Translation is not math, it's art with a hint of math.

Whether in the Psalms or not, when you run across a problematic text or one that just seems puzzling to you, a good first step if you are not a student of the biblical languages (and while I have studied them in my distant past, I would characterize myself as highly reliant on the work of translators) is to visit a few other translations to see if any greater clarity can be found there.

Back to farming faithfulness. I put out a few tomato plants, one cucumber and one green pepper this spring. The cucumbers showed up first, a couple of green peppers have appeared, and the tomatoes are beginning to ripen. I really don't know if they would taste better to me in a blind taste test, but with my eyes wide open, picking them from the vine, washing them and preparing them I think the ones from the backyard are amazing.

The image of "farming faithfulness" puts me in the mind of digging around in our spiritual lives – working with scripture, prayer, worship, acts of kindness and care to see what sorts of spiritual fruits and vegetables begin to turn up. I love the organic feel of the idea and the way it points to a necessary commitment. Faith is not waiting for magic to happen, it's farming faithfulness.

Prayer

My farming is not spectacular. Help me to be better at it, making use of all the resources that you have provided to help me in the work. Amen.

Day 14

Psalms 39, 40, 41

As we reach Psalm 41, we reach the end of the first of the five books within the Psalter. The five book structure seems likely to have been an homage to the five books of the Torah.

Psalm 40 begins with praise and thanksgiving for answered prayer.

I put all my hope in the Lord.
He leaned down to me;
 he listened to my cry for help.
He lifted me out of the pit of death,
 out of the mud and filth,
 and set my feet on solid rock.
He steadied my legs. (40:1-2)

The praise for answered prayer quickly becomes a renewed crisis, a new sense of danger and a new prayer asking for God's intervention.

"...my courage leaves me.
Favor me, Lord, and deliver me!" (12-13)

It sounds dramatic because of the poetic language, but this could describe any day of the week in most of our lives. We experience a blessing and we offer a prayer of thanksgiving. We continue with our day, a problem presents itself, anything from a snag in the day to a chasm in our heart, and we are back before God, confessing that our courage has gone on holiday once again.

The poem resolves in a place of hope as we are reminded that we bring our needs before God who is more than capable of meeting any circumstance that comes along.

"But me? I'm weak and needy.

Let my Lord think of me.

You are my help and my rescuer.

My God, don't wait any longer!" (17)

Prayer

When my strength is waning and my courage is lacking, turn me once again towards you and the hope I have in you, my God, my help, my rescuer. Amen.

Day 15

Psalms 42, 43, 44

Have you ever noticed that while you need water to live you are not thirsty all the time? We are encouraged by folks interested in our health and well-being to be sure and drink enough water each day, even suggesting ways of reminding ourselves to drink a set amount of water at different times throughout the day.

As a runner I notice my thirst most after a long run. I like coffee and Coke Zero, but in the moment after a long run there is nothing like cold water. I suspect you know what it's like to reach that moment when what you want more than anything is a simple thirst quenching drink of water. Nothing else will satisfy in that moment like the simple gift of water.

Psalm 42 reminds us that our relationship with God can be like this. We need God or our lives will not be what they are intended to be. And yet our lives are not consumed 24/7 with a search for God. That's not a critique, it's a statement of reality. What's also true though is that there are times when we become as acutely aware of our need for God as a thirsty person does of their need for water.

"Just like a deer that craves

streams of water,

my whole being craves you, God.

My whole being thirsts for God,

for the living God.

When will I come and see God's face?" (42:1)

In her poem "Thirsting," inspired by this Psalm, Julia Seymour writes,

"The parching of my soul comes from my own failure to drink

from the fountain of all blessings.

I wander down my own path with just a few things to finish before...

and then something comes up...

and after dinner, I will...

tend to other things crowding my mind."[1]

Let's listen to the psalmist's call to tend to our parched souls.

Prayer

Thank you for living water that sustains. Inspire me to drink deeply. Amen.

---

[1] Seymour, Julia, "Thirsting," *The Words of Her Mouth: Psalms for the Struggle*, Martha Spong, ed., Pilgrim Press, 2020, 42.

Week Four

Psalms 45-61

Day 16
Psalms 45, 46, 47, 48

Day 17
Psalms 49, 50

Day 18
Psalms 51, 52, 53, 54

Day 19
Psalms 55, 56, 57

Day 20
Psalms 58, 59, 60, 61

"Create a clean heart for me, God;
put a new, faithful spirit deep inside me!"
-Psalm 51:10

Day 16

Psalms 45, 46, 47, 48

When I was a boy my family would make an annual trip to King's Island, an amusement park just outside of Cincinnati. This was a big deal. The visual centerpiece of Kings Island is a one-third scale replica of the Eiffel Tower. My sister and I would watch to see who could spot the landmark first as we drew closer to the park. When we saw it, rising gloriously before us, there was excitement and great rejoicing - a day of fun was about to begin.

The first time I flew into a New York City airport, my eyes were focused out the window taking in the amazing cityscape, but looking in particular for the Statue of Liberty holding aloft her torch and bidding welcome. After seeing it in books, on TV and in movies, there it was, standing in the harbor just below Manhattan! It was exciting to see something so familiar in person for the first time.

The most memorable experience like this that I have ever had occurred when my wife, Julie, and I took our first trip to the Holy Land. Driving into Jerusalem the first time was not entirely unlike driving into any major city. Lots of traffic. Lots of buildings and houses. And then we came over a hill and the Old City of Jerusalem unfolded before us.

It was early evening, dusk, the lights of the city were on, and it was magnificent. There were the walls built by the Sultan Suleiman in the 1500's. There was the Dome of the Rock built on the Temple Mount. There were the gray domes of the Church of the Holy Sepulcher. It was breathtaking.

Psalm 48 reminds me of that moment of my first glimpse of the Holy City and subsequently the emotions of walking through the streets within its walls.

"In the city belonging to our God,
   the Lord is great
   and so is worthy of praise!
His holy mountain is a beautiful summit,
   the joy of the whole world.
Mount Zion, in the far north
   is the city of the great king.
God is in its fortifications,
   revealing himself as a place of safety." (48:1-2)

It's stunning to consider that the place we drove into with a bus full of pilgrims in February of 2000 is the same place the psalmist describes with such joy and to imagine that while more than two thousand years have passed since those words were written, the view can still inspire the same feeling today.

Prayer

Thank you for places near and far that fill us with joy and inspire thoughts of holiness. Amen.

Jerusalem - The Old City from the Mount of Olives

Day 17

Psalms 49, 50

These two Psalms work side by side nicely. Psalm 49 spells out the depth and the height of the reach of God's words to the world:

"Listen to this, all you people!

Listen closely, all you citizens of the world -

people of every kind, rich and poor

alike." (49:1-2)

Psalm 50 speaks of the majesty of God:

"From the rising of the sun to where it sets,

God, the Lord God, speaks,

calling out to the earth.

From Zion, perfect in beauty,

God shines brightly." (50:1-2)

The things we use to divide ourselves up, in particular the ways we use wealth or the lack of wealth to measure a person's worth are trivial in God's sight and in reality don't mean so much to us over the long haul. Regardless of our net worth we have the one life to experience God's world and to know others and build relationships. What we collect and accumulate along the way will not be going with us to the grave.

There is something of the book of Proverbs here and also hints of the book of Ecclesiastes, with its assertion that all is vanity.

Psalm 50 is a logical companion in its assertion that God is not impressed with the stuff that is brought to be sacrificed to God - God doesn't need another cow - but rather honors the offering of true thanksgiving and praise. The focus here is on getting our perspective right. If we find ourselves living to impress and outdo each other it will lead to unhappiness and a continual feeling that we need to do more and add more. If we can wrap our minds around the truth that what is most valued from us by the One who created everything is relationship with us we have the best path to a healthy relationship with God and with one another.

"The one who offers
  a sacrifice of thanksgiving
  is the one who honors me.
 And it is to the one who charts
  the correct path that I will show
  divine salvation." (50:23)

Prayer

When I start chasing after stuff, slow me down and remind me of what is important. Teach me again and again to chase after you, and to value and treat as your children the people you place in my path each day. Amen.

Day 18

Psalms 51, 52, 53, 54

Two associations come to mind when I read Psalm 51. First, it is connected by the editor of the Psalms with the story of David, Uriah and Bathsheba and the subsequent prophetic word from Nathan to David. This is presented as David's internal struggle with his sin and his need for God's mercy. Second, Psalm 51 has always been a part of Ash Wednesday services for many folks and always for services I have led. I have stood before many people over the years and imposed ashes with words adapted from this text.

"Create a clean heart for me, God;

   put a new, faithful spirit deep inside me!" (51:10)

Sin can impact our minds in a variety of ways. It can make us sad and fill us with despair. It can cause us to fear God's judgment and anticipate God's punishment. It can lead us to want to do better, recognizing our failings and wanting very much to not repeat them again and again. In his commentary on this chapter, Derek Kidner[1] points out that the language here is hopeful.

---

[1] Kidner, Derek. *Psalms 1-72 (Tyndale Old Testament Commentaries)*, InterVarsity Press, 1973, 209.

"And yes, you want truth
   in the most hidden places;
   you teach me wisdom
   in the most secret space." (51:6)

Kidner sees God portrayed in this way - "desiring truth he will teach...wisdom, not deplore its absence." What a blessing when we can be honest with God, trusting that God's interest is not destroying us for the wrongs we have done, but teaching us a better way to live going forward.

Prayer

Create in me a clean heart, O God, and put a new and right spirit within me. Make me teachable. Heal my broken spirit that I may aim again to serve you. Amen.

Day 19

Psalms 55, 56, 57

We cannot quit racism. No matter how many times we say that this is not who we are or who we want to be, we, as a society, produce another example that tells our truth. Yes, it is not our whole truth, but it is a persistently present thread of our truth here in North America for the past four hundred years.

In the wake of another act of violence on video, I have seen many black leaders on television who simply look and sound tired. Filled with pain, frustrated, angry, hurting, and weary. Each of the Psalms for today, particularly 55 and 56 as I read them, have language which speaks of the weariness I see.

Part of it is a weariness of enough is enough:

"God, listen to my prayer;

Don't avoid my request!

Pay attention! Answer me!" (55:1)

There is also the weariness of simply wanting to transcend this present circumstance:

"I wish I had wings like a dove!

I'd fly away and rest.

I'd run so far away!

54

I'd live in the desert.

I'd hurry to my hideout,

 far from the rushing wind and storms." (55:6-8)

There is a beautiful portion of Psalm 57 which yearns for a bright tomorrow.

"My heart is unwavering, God-

 my heart is unwavering.

 I will sing and make music.

 Wake up, my glory!

 Wake up, harp and lyre!

 I will wake the dawn itself!" (57:7-8)

I want for our world to be better and to do better. I want for my country to be better and do better. For me it has to begin with me seeking God's help in being better and doing better in my life and my sphere of influence. I do not want to be quietly acquiescent, wishing that this is not who I am. I want to invite God to challenge and change me and help me to grow so that I can join my voice along with so many others that are seeking to move past the night to wake the dawn itself.

Prayer

Forgive me. Help me to grow and to be better. Help us towards a world where the joyous morning of waking up is truly joyous for all. Amen.

Day 20

Psalms 58, 59, 60, 61

One of the great treats of the summers of childhood was visiting a community swimming pool. There was a swim test that had to be successfully completed before one was allowed to swim in the deep end. The deep end was of course home to the diving board, which was largely the motivation to take the test.

I remember hanging out near the rope that separated the shallow end from the deep end, wondering what it was like to be in a place where water was all around and your feet wouldn't touch the bottom. I was pretty sure I could swim the needed distance to pass the test, but for awhile I wasn't sure if I could do it in the deep end without the safety net of being able to stand up. The distance was the same, but the depth made all the difference in the mental calculation.

There are moments in life where we realize we aren't in the shallow end anymore. Difficulties and challenges come all at once and when we go to stand up to get our breath the only option is to tread water as best we can. Treading water can be exhausting. I think of all that when I read these words from Psalm 61.

"Lead me to the rock

   that is higher than I am

   because you have been my refuge

   a tower of strength

   in the face of the enemy. (61:2-3)

This is exactly the kind of prayer we pray when the waters of life are tossing us around and feel like they may overtake us. Get me to higher ground, Lord! Experience has taught me that God will do exactly that. Often it's not a miraculous rescue - the situation doesn't dissolve into peace with nothing more to be done - instead it's a support, a time to get oriented and catch my breath before returning to the troubled waters with renewed strength for the journey. File this verse away for those times when the water seems to be rising and what you most need is a moment of rest to breathe deeply and freely.

Prayer

There is a lot of deep end swimming required in life Holy God. Thank you for lifting me up when I need to breathe. Amen.

Week Five

Psalms 62-74

Day 21
Psalms 62, 63, 64, 65

Day 22
Psalms 66, 67, 68

Day 23
Psalms 69, 70

Day 24
Psalms 71, 72

Day 25
Psalms 73, 74

"But me?
My prayer reaches you, Lord,
at just the right time."
-Psalm 69:13

Day 21

Psalms 62, 63, 64, 65

This group of Psalms worked like a quartet for me as I read them today. The way a great piece of music will develop several themes and allow them to work upon each other, the themes of being silent and finding rest in God exist here alongside of contemplation on God's greatness and on the futility of imagining we can have secrets from the One who made us.

Psalm 62 deftly lifts out the unique character of God; it is only in God that rest can be found. Psalm 64 questions why we so often - rather than seeking to embrace that rest - aim to evade God through futile attempts at secrecy:

> "'Let someone try to expose our crimes!
> We've devised a perfect plot!
> It's deep within the human mind and heart.'
> But God will shoot them
> with an arrow!
> Without warning,
> they will be wounded!" (64:6-7)

So much energy is invested in plots and plans to throw God off our true intentions or plans. Like an arrow finding its target, God's vision reaches into our innermost beings. Why hide when what God wants to offer is rest and communion?

Psalm 65 offers the broadest possible canvas so that we may see that the theatre in which we play out our days is entirely the work of God. We can imagine distant places. There are no distant places for God. The setting of the sun and its return in the morning are mysteries we cannot orchestrate, but it is all within God's creative activity.

"You make the gateways

 Of morning and evening sing for joy." (65:8)

The net effect of this symphony is to point out the futility of running from God who has called everything into being, knows us better than we know ourselves, and invites us, even as we are mired in chaos, to find peace and rest.

Prayer

Today is Monday, the gateway of morning into a new week. Help me this week to hide less and rest more in you. Amen.

Day 22

Psalms 66, 67, 68

This text is a good reminder that reading scripture with a solid commentary on hand can be helpful. In this instance, Psalm 68 is opened up a bit by consulting the work of biblical scholars. It has been suggested that this Psalm was perhaps a part of the liturgy surrounding the carrying of the Ark of the Covenant into the Temple. This is not a "for certain" thing, but where does the idea come from at all? To begin with, from the opening line of the poem. It is a quotation of Numbers 10:35, wherein Moses is quoted amidst a description of the people marching with the Ark.

Further on the psalmist dips back a couple of times to the book of Judges and quotes from the Song of Deborah (Judges 5). This occurs in v.13 and v.38. Knowing this can make us curious about why the writer might choose to quote from these older poems at this point in time. Is there any illumination offered for the Psalm in understanding the context of the earlier texts. Sometimes the answer may be a clear yes - other times not so certainly, but often it is worth exploration.

Finally today a nod to Psalm 66:13-14:

"I'll keep the promises I made to you,

  the ones my lips uttered,

  the ones my mouth spoke

  when I was in deep trouble."

Bargaining with God clearly has a long history. These words from the distant past of our faith could easily be spoken by any one of us today who has in a tough spot made a promise to God, fully intending in that moment, to keep it.

Prayer

Thank you for scripture that speaks your truth to us and thank you for those who have studied its languages and history to bring further light to our own reading. Amen.

Day 23

Psalms 69, 70

The sense of urgency is immediate in Psalm 70:

"Hurry, God, to deliver me;
   hurry, Lord, to help me!" (70:1)

When it feels like the sky is falling, when disaster is imminent, when what we dread feels certain to be around the next corner we want God to stand up and take notice right then. Please don't be on break right now God. Act. Save me.

Contrast this with the experience of the poet in Psalm 69:

"But me? My prayer reaches you, Lord,
   at just the right time." (69:13)

The message here seems to be that God experience has indicated that God will act when God will act and that action will come in time. So which approach is right? I'd suggest both of them. I'd love to say my trust has matured to the point that I never feel the crush of uncertainty, that I always practice the patience of waiting on the Lord. I don't.

I wholeheartedly believe that God long ago convinced me that God's faithfulness and timing are beyond reproach. I have complete confidence in that truth. And I still find some version of "hurry" showing up in my prayers on a regular basis. The Psalms teach us not to edit ourselves in conversation with God. God's timing will be God's timing, but in our interaction I think God values honesty and sometimes nothing will more honestly convey my heart than imploring God to hurry.

Prayer

I trust, O God, that your timing is perfect. Forgive me, but I'm still going to ask you to hurry sometimes. Amen.

Day 24

Psalms 71, 72

In his book "How To Pray", Pete Greig[1] speaks about times when "adoration fails to erupt spontaneously" in his prayer life. "This is an act of will. Instead of waiting to worship until I feel like it (which could be a very long wait indeed), I begin to thank God for all the evidence of his love in my life - often speaking out loud - until my feelings fall into line with the facts."

This sentiment came to mind when I read Psalm 71.

"My mouth will repeat

Your righteous acts

And your saving deeds all day long.

I don't even know

How many of those there are." (71:15)

This discipline of rehearsing the blessings of God that we experience in our lives each day is a great way, as Greig argues, to keep our hearts primed for praising God.

---

[1] Greig, Pete. *How to Pray: A Simple Guide for Normal People*, NavPress, 2019, 59.

The troubles and complications of particular days can distract us from all that God does on our behalf. They can cause us to discount the blessings of God which the psalmist reminds us are impossible to number.

Already today I am thankful for maple pecan coffee, uplifting words from friends, playful interactions between cardinals and house finches at my bird feeder, and a message from a church member that a medical procedure is past and recovery is underway. What blessings are you counting today? How will you keep your hope always before you?

Prayer

Source of hope and giver of all good gifts, fill my heart with gratitude and keep me ready to offer you thanks and praise. Amen.

Day 25

Psalms 73, 74

The saying about the grass being greener on the other side of the fence is one that exists explicitly to remind us that such thinking is an illusion. Things may look great over there, but generally the other side of the fence has its own set of problems.

Very often it is not so much that we love the other side as we are unhappy with something about our side. We imagine that we lack in some way. It appears that things are newer and better over there.

The next step - the step taken by the psalmist in Psalm 73 - is to begin to look at the people over there and find their flaws. They are undeserving. They have not worked as hard as we have. Things are easier for them because they have more resources. There may be grains of truth in some of our observations, but they don't really help us to do anything but get jealous and angry. And, remember, often it's not actually true. While things may be better in some observable ways over there than on our side, there are struggles and shortcomings and failures over there as well.

Once more the Psalms are a safe place to be honest with God about how we are hurting and about what we may be experiencing as inequities. It can perhaps be a productive thing to place all the pain and the longing on the table and ask God to help us with hard questions. And then it is a good thing to listen for God. To be reminded of God's faithfulness, and to be reoriented to how God has blessed us and moved to offer God praise.

"It's good for me to be near God.

I have taken my refuge in you,

My Lord God,

So I can talk all about your works!" (73:28)

Prayer

The world is a gift filled with your blessings. It is not a warehouse with a finite supply and most of it already gone to someone else. Help me to see your gifts and rejoice in your blessings. Amen.

Week Six

Psalms 75-88

Day 26
Psalms 75, 76, 77

Day 27
Psalm 78

Day 28
Psalms 79, 80, 81

Day 29
Psalms 82, 83, 84, 85

Day 30
Psalms 86, 87, 88

"Better is a single day in your courtyards
than a thousand days anywhere else!"
-Psalm 84:10

Day 26
Psalms 75, 76, 77

In Psalm 76:2 Jerusalem is referred to as Salem. This echoes back to the earliest biblical reference to Jerusalem in Genesis 14:18. There we find mention of a King Melchizedek of Salem. King Melchizedek was around long before the days of the united monarchy, prior to any hint of what the Holy City would become. It does give an indication of the long history of civilization in that location.

In my visits as a pilgrim/tourist I have found the Old City of Jerusalem to be a place where things spiritual seem almost tangible. The muezzin call to prayer audible five times a day throughout the city. The distinctive garb of the Orthodox Jews. The bus loads of Christian pilgrims. And in the Old City. The Dome of the Rock atop the Temple Mount. The Western or Wailing Wall - a retaining wall of Herod's Temple. The gray domes of the Church of the Holy Sepulcher, which houses the traditional location of the crucifixion and the resurrection of Christ.

To imagine that once upon a time there was a King Melchizedek in a tiny Kingdom called Salem around that location. That it would become under David's leadership the capital of the United Kingdom of Israel. That it would from that time on be a spot of great faith and great tumult.

I don't believe that God is contained in any particular place, or that God dwells in any one location - as Psalm 76:2 suggests. However, I must also confess that earth seems very near to the heavens in that square mile or so around Mount Zion. It is a fitting setting for soaring language like that found in Psalm 72 and so many other of these ancient poems.

Prayer

Thank you for stories of your making yourself known to your people in places on the map that exist to this day. Because you were there we know you do not keep yourself far removed from your people, but can also be here where we are as well. Amen.

Day 27

Psalm 78

A lot of discussion in Sunday School and Bible studies has gone into dealing with the circumstance of prayer in which God's answer seems to be no. That is, what to do when we ask God for something specifically to happen and it does not. There is a lot of fruit on that tree from the perspective of having a healthy discussion - people who have prayed a lot have at some point, probably several points, earnestly prayed for something which did not wind up with the hoped for outcome.

On the other hand, I am not sure I remember a conversation about what we do when prayer turns out exactly in the way in which we had hoped. What do we do when God says yes? The obvious answer might be that we celebrate what has happened and go forward with enthusiasm and ever-increasing faith.

Not so fast.

Psalm 78 is a remembrance of God's deliverance of the people from Egypt and providential care while they were in the wilderness.

When they were thirsty they asked for water and God provided water from a rock. When they were hungry they asked God for food and God rained manna from heaven.

To be clear, the asking part involved a people newly liberated by God complaining loudly to Moses that things had been better in Egypt and had Moses brought them out to the wilderness to die. Moses had then interceded with God on their behalf and their prayers were answered in somewhat miraculous ways. But it was not enough.

"So they ate and were completely satisfied;

God gave them exactly

What they had craved;

But they didn't stop craving - Even with the food still in their mouths!" (78:29-30)

Rather than celebration and praise, the response to prayers miraculously answered in the affirmative was to begin wanting the next thing even as they were enjoying the last thing. The point here isn't to throw the people in the wilderness under the bus, but to shine a light on a problem that can afflict us as well. Prayer is often more like an ongoing conversation and answer unfolding slowly over time. Sometimes the yes or no of an answer takes some time to tease out. The caution here is that our human nature sometimes fails to allow us to be satisfied with yes.

When we experience God's blessings in our lives, when our prayers are answered and the answer looks much like a yes to what we were praying for - in other words when it should be easiest for us to celebrate and give thanks we miss out on a glorious opportunity to worship and be present with the One who has blessed us when we rush on ahead to whatever is next on our list.

Prayer

Slow me down. Open my eyes. Help me to be grateful. Thank you for all that you are, all that you have done, are doing and will do in the future. Amen.

Day 28

Psalms 79, 80, 81

Have you ever felt lost? Disoriented? Uprooted from the familiar and dear to you, and set down in a new place that you do not understand? There is a tender description in the midst of Psalm 81 of what life was like for the Hebrew people when they were in slavery in Egypt. The psalmist says, "I heard a language I did not yet know." (81:5) That's a vivid and jarring description of feeling out of step with ones surroundings.

Over the span of history covered by the Psalms this feeling occurs multiple times for the Hebrew people. Beyond the bondage in Egypt there was the fall of the northern kingdom of Israel, followed around one hundred and forty years later by the fall of Judah. The Psalms and the entire Old Testament are filled with situations where the people found themselves - in Egypt, Assyria, Babylon, and more - hearing a language they did not yet know.

This sort of disruption and disorientation continues to be a part of life to this day. In large scale ways we know our world today is filled with people who have been uprooted from one place and forced to seek out refuge somewhere else.

The suffering of large populations of people who simply seek out a safe place to make a life with their families is a phenomena that is happening in too many places around our world.

This can be a very personal struggle as well. Individuals can slip quietly into despair for a variety of reasons. The loss of a job and subsequent change of economic circumstances. The illness or death of a loved one and the accompanying sense of being cast adrift in a sea of anxiety and grief. Even changes that appear to be positive can be challenging when they bring new places, people and ways of being into our routine.

Many of the Psalms offer helpful exploration of this dynamic. They give voice to our questions and concerns. They help us to know that others have shared the struggle of finding a way in new, often difficult, and even painful circumstances. They offer comfort, reminding us that God is with us when life seems to be speaking a language we do not yet know.

Prayer

We give thanks, our Good Shepherd, for your guidance and presence even when we feel lost. Help us to listen for your familiar voice in those times when all seems unfamiliar and we feel lost. Call our names and help us to trust that you never give up on us. Amen.

Day 29

Psalms 82, 83, 84, 85

The first time I went to the Holy Land I imagined I was going as a religious tourist - I hadn't given it a lot of thought. The opportunity came to go and I went. It changed me. I have returned multiple times and since that first trip have understood the journey to be something other than tourism - it is a pilgrimage. This has led me to explore the background of pilgrimage and take time to consider how waking up in the morning and journeying through the day is, in its own way, a pilgrimage.

In the very helpful book *The Pilgrim's Compass: Finding and Following the God We Seek*,[1] Paul Lang writes, "Again and again the biblical faith is shaped and transformed by the practice of journeying in response to God's call - pilgrimage."

Psalm 84 is a pilgrimage Psalm. It speaks of the people's literal journey from the Judean countryside to worship at the Temple and of their spiritual journey from everyday life to standing in the presence of God.

"As they pass through the Baca Valley,

---

[1] Lang, Paul. *The Pilgrim's Compass: Finding And Following The God We Seek*, Westminster John Knox Press, 2019, 11.

they make it a spring of water.
Yes, the early rain covers it
 with blessings.
They go from strength to strength
until they see the supreme God in Zion." (84:6-7)
"Better is a single day in your courtyards
 than a thousand days anywhere else!" (84:10)

Pilgrimage is Abraham setting out for a place, not knowing where he is going. It is the people following Moses into uncertainty in the wilderness. It is the faithful coming from all over the land to worship in Jerusalem in the times of the monarchy and on forward to the time of Christ.

Pilgrimage is us today, heading out the door in the morning to walk and pray and seek God's presence. Our faith is, as Lang suggests, shaped and transformed as we journey literally and spiritually in response to God's call. As we put one foot in front of the other we are reminded that just as this is how we move from one point to another, this is also how we draw closer to God, step by step, pilgrims in this life. Lang once more: "Faith as pilgrimage is thus both the daily practice of discipleship and the journey to a place of hope-filled and expectant encounter."

Blessed travels fellow pilgrims!

Prayer

Empower me to hear and to heed your call. Keep me marching to Zion. Amen.

Day 30

Psalms 86, 87, 88

We know Jesus made a habit of going off by himself, or perhaps accompanied by a small group of followers, to pray. Sometimes it is early in the morning, sometimes in the evening, but whatever the time of day there is clearly a pattern.

We know that Jesus was familiar with the Psalms. The Psalms are a part of the fabric of his teaching and he sometimes quotes them directly. They are an important part of his vocabulary of conversation when he prays.

We know that Jesus' prayer life was intrinsically tied up with what was happening in his life at any given moment. The ultimate example being his prayer in the garden of Gethsemane on the night before his crucifixion. Jesus was deeply troubled and he prays the prayer of a deeply troubled individual.

All of this is to say, I thought of Jesus a lot as I read Psalm 88. I wonder if he ever found himself early in the morning on a hill next to the Sea of Galilee before sunrise using this language:

"But I cry out to you Lord!
My prayer meets you
First thing in the morning!" (88:14)

I'm imagining Jesus not perfunctorily pulling himself from slumber to satisfy his morning obligations, but heading out in the morning with great need and anticipation, praying about next steps for his work and care and provision for himself and his disciples. Psalm 88 is not a bright, ebullient Psalm of praise. It's heavy and hard and earnest. Perhaps on some Galilean mornings it was the heaviness of his call that drove Jesus to pray.

Psalm 88 is yet another place where the Psalms are inviting us to be open and honest with God. To put on the table the things that weigh on us and keep us awake at night. Clearly there are moments for praise and worship, but there is never a need to paper over our uncertainty and pain when in the presence of our God.

Prayer

Whether morning, noon or night, I give thanks that you listen to me when I am joyful and filled with praise and when I am hurting and filled with distress. You welcome it all and are always ready to listen. Amen.

Week Seven

Psalms 89-104

Day 31
Psalm 89

Day 32
Psalms 90, 91, 92, 93

Day 33
Psalms 94, 95, 96, 97

Day 34
Psalms 98, 99, 100, 101, 102

Day 35
Psalms 103, 104

"Sing to the Lord a new song
because he has done
wonderful things."
-Psalm 98:1

Day 31

Psalm 89

Psalm 89 is epic in length which is appropriate because it is epic in content as well. Among the themes are the singular, unique greatness of God, the joys of covenant relationship with God, the perils of breaking covenant, and, for spice, reflection on the brush stroke made by the fleeting nature of a human life on the canvas of all of history. It's a lot.

There are clues throughout this Psalm reminding us that it is virtually impossible for us to talk about or understand God in the abstract. How powerful is God? Powerful enough to rule over the sea and crush sea monsters. How awesome is God's creation? God made both Mt. Tabor and Mt. Hermon. How much does God love God's people? God called forth a gifted leader, David, to inspire and defend them.

This leads us to the importance of finding ways to connect the greatness of God with things in our everyday experience.

How powerful is God? Powerful enough to help us persevere through a pandemic. How awesome is God's creation? Living in the beautiful Bluegrass State I have plenty of places to look for answers. How much does God love God's people? I can point to the congregation I serve - so many people who have gifted me with multiple examples of God's love.

Today is a good day to join with the psalmist and sing of the Lord's loyal love forever, proclaiming God's faithfulness at every opportunity.

Prayer

I will sing of your love this day and proclaim your faithfulness. Help me to keep this promise. Amen.

Day 32

Psalms 90, 91, 92, 93

Psalm 90 kicks off the fourth book within the Psalms with a jarring poem about the fleeting nature of human life set alongside the timeless nature of God.

"Before the mountains were born,
   before you birthed the earth
   and the inhabited world-
   from forever in the past
   to forever in the future, you are God.
 You return people to dust,
   saying, 'Go back, humans,'
   because in your perspective
   a thousand years
   are like yesterday past,
   like a short period
   during the night watch." (90:1-4)

I enjoy walking in the cemetery across the street from the church I pastor. There are a number of the saints of our church who have gone on to the church triumphant buried there, familiar names etched into the stones, prompting me to greet them as I walk past.

Some pre-date my time as pastor, but I know their names from the stories of long-time members and from plaques on pews and walls. Some are folks I have known and loved and journeyed with and as I walk I imagine our journey continues as I get my steps in the presence of the great cloud of witnesses.

My embrace and commitment to my walking habit was born of my diagnosis as diabetic several years back. Perhaps ironically, I walk amongst the tombstones as a means of staying healthy. The cemetery is not a sad place. It is a restful place, an inspiring place even. It is a place that forcibly grants perspective. "Teach us to number our days" indeed.

Here again is the grandeur of the Psalms. A book of hymns spoken into a world that looked very little like the one we walk around in, yet also very much like it, as we strive to make meaning of our lives on the sweeping canvas of God's forever.

Prayer

Thank you for the opportunity to walk through your world. Remind me when I am impatient that for you "a thousand years are like yesterday past" - make me grateful for each beautiful moment. Amen.

Day 33

Psalms 94, 95, 96, 97

We all have the bait we cannot refuse. The trouble we cannot walk past without stopping. One of these for me is the suggestion that things are worse now than they have ever been. It usually comes up gathered around tables in a discussion, informally or in a study setting, with the momentum building as the list of the vagaries of the day grows longer and longer. This must, the line of thinking concludes, be as bad as the world has ever been.

Maybe. But I don't think so. And I can't help responding. Every time.

We did not perfect sin and evil, we are just the current practitioners. This whole range of Psalms features language about God as king, ruling over the creation. A king whose judgement will carry the day, the real and true God who will emerge from the pretenders who are all idols or "ungods" as Robert Alter[1] suggests.

---

[1] Alter, Robert. *The Book of Psalms: A Translation With Commentary*, W. W. Norton & Company, 2007, 339.

It is most likely an argument without a point. Whether or not we win for being the ugliest and most repugnant, we can certainly hold our own. My motivation in attending to the fight is to oppose the idea that our progression into darkness points towards the curtain falling on the creation. In our linear sense of things we, I guess, must be closer to the end than the beginning, but trying to anticipate what that end might look like and when it will occur are activities I resist.

The psalmist reminds that above the wicked ways of any particular historical moment, God reigns. Whether it is the arrogant and wicked of ancient times or the internet trolls and self-serving of the present, God corrects us, asks more of us and is worthy of our praise.

"Come, let's sing out loud to the Lord!

Let's raise a joyful shout

To the rock of our salvation!" (95:1)

Prayer

I am sinful enough without trying to place myself on the historical continuum of disobedience. Forgive me and call me to worship you O rock of my salvation. Amen.

Day 34

Psalms 98, 99, 100, 101, 102

I think worship is a good way to begin to get my hands around what I will never fully understand. I am capable of considering the word holy, but I can truly fashion only the vaguest understanding of what the word means. Psalms 98-101 each offer some assistance in building a vocabulary of holiness. If there are times when you might have trouble imagining singing some of these poems, here is the place to look for several that don't require much work in picturing the people lifting their voices in praise.

"Magnify the Lord our God!
  Bow low at his holy mountain
    because the Lord our God is holy!" (99:9)
"Sing to the Lord a new song
  because he has done
    wonderful things." (98:1)
"Oh let me sing
  about faithful love and justice!
  I want to sing my praises to you, Lord!" (101:1)

These songs remind me of the great hymns of Easter. I have preached more than twenty Easter sermons, led many Maundy Thursday and Good Friday services and had that many more conversations in studies, Sunday School and informal conversations about the resurrection. Point being it's been a part of my faith and practically speaking a part of my work to think about it and talk about it. And I could not begin to explain what happened between that last meal and the empty tomb.

How did it happen? What exactly happened? How many words, would you need? The closest I think I come to understanding it is probably when we sing "Christ The Lord Is Risen Today", the soaring music, the unbridled joy.

The holiness of God is like that. There is a time to write, to talk, to listen and to speak. And there is a time to join our voices together and sing and maybe even shout.

"Shout triumphantly to the Lord
All the earth.
Be happy!
Rejoice out loud!
Sing your praises!" (98:4)

Prayer

Your holiness is greater than my imagination. Thank you for song to give voice to what is beyond my understanding. Amen.

Day 35

Psalms 103, 104

Psalms 103 and 104 begin and end pretty much the same way.

"Let my whole being bless the Lord!
 Let everything inside me
  bless his holy name!" (103:1)
"All God's creatures,
  bless the Lord!
 Everywhere, throughout his kingdom,
  let my whole being
  bless the Lord!" (103:22)

"Let my whole being, bless the Lord!
 Lord my God, how fantastic you are!
 You are clothed in glory and grandeur!" (104:1)
"Let sinners be wiped clean
 From the earth;
 Let the wicked be no more.
 But let my whole being bless the Lord!
 Praise the Lord!" (104:35)

There have been perhaps fragments of moments when it has felt as though my whole being was praising the Lord. Moments. Filled with thankfulness. Filled with a sense of the immensity of God's grace. Overwhelmed with being loved or with the surprising capacity to love. But they are fleeting moments.

Then comes back the irritations. The grudges. The frustrations with myself. The daunting nature of the tenacity of all the things that want to fill my being and my sense of my own rebellion at times running towards those competitors for my attention rather than fighting to focus on God.

It would be no small thing to get my whole being to do anything. It would be glorious to turn my whole being to living out each day blessing the Lord.

Prayer

So often what I experience as the brokenness of sin begins with where I focus my whole being. Today help me seek a moment to focus my whole being on you and see what follows from that. Amen.

Week Eight

Psalms 105-116

Day 36
Psalm 105

Day 37
Psalm 106

Day 38
Psalms 107, 108

Day 39
Psalms 109, 110, 111, 112

Day 40
Psalms 113, 114, 115, 116

"Pursue the Lord and his strength;
Seek his face always."
-Psalm 105:5

Day 36

Psalm 105

Psalm 105 opens with a few introductory verses and then turns to specific examples of God's faithfulness in the covenant relationship with Israel. Verse 7 through the end of the chapter take us from the earliest patriarchs through the entry into the promised land.

I'm drawn today to the first six verses. It is a general call/invitation to the people to be in an open and ready to give and receive stance towards God. The first word(s) of the first five verses give the cues on how to do this.

Give thanks. Sing. Give praise.

Pursue. Remember.

That is a lot of effective education in the practice of faith in a short space. Each of the first three point us towards gratitude, reverence and joyous praise. They invite us to orient ourselves properly to our Creator. As in Jesus' teaching in the Lord's Prayer (hallowed be thy name), the approach to God begins with acknowledgement of the greatness of God.

Of the five, I am most intrigued by pursuit.

"Pursue the Lord and his strength;
 Seek his face always." (105:5)

We are not directed to wait for life to happen to and around us and to ferret out as best we can in the aftermath where God might have been involved. We are to pursue God.

Robert Alter's translation[1] uses the word "inquire", which suggests an attitude of questioning. I like the combination of both words - setting off at the start of the day to pursue where God is going and where we should be following along with a curiosity that leads us to boldly and expectantly, like a small child in the backseat of the car asking how long till we get there and where exactly is there?

Remembering is, ironically, one of our best sources of hope. We receive inspiration for tomorrow, by reminding ourselves what God has done in all our yesterdays. Whatever tomorrow looks like, God has always been faithful and God's promises are to be trusted.

Prayer

Help me to express my thanks. Hear me when I lift my voice in songs and in praise. Make me eager to pursue you and your will. Remind me that following you has always proven to be a great idea. Amen.

---

[1] Alter, Robert. *The Book of Psalms: A Translation With Commentary*, W. W. Norton & Company, 2007, 369.

Day 37

Psalm 106

Some scholars believe Psalm 106 is a companion Psalm to Psalm 105. If not composed as a companion piece it is at least no accident that they rest next to one another at the end of Book IV of the Psalms. They are each lengthy historical poems, both recounting the days of Israel's liberation from Egypt and the repeated mighty acts of God to save them in the wilderness and ultimately lead them to their new home. What varies is the perspective.

Psalm 105 tells the story as a hymn of praise to God for all the places along the way where God acted on behalf of the people. It remembers with joy to inspire hope for the future. Psalm 106 tells the story as a cautionary tale. It remembers the repeated response of the people to God's actions as lacking in gratitude and revealing natures that are repeatedly dissatisfied with miraculous deliverance, craving more even as the previous craving is being satisfied. Midway through Psalm 106 we are told:

"So our ancestors trusted God's words;

they sang God's praise.

But how quickly they forgot what he had done." (106:12-13)

This is a not looking to the past with joy to inspire hope for the future. This is looking to the future with an eye for scarcity and lack, distrusting the faithfulness of God at every turn in their past. Same story. Different choice of how to live with it.

In the first[2] of Louise Penny's *Inspector Gamache* novels, the Inspector is imparting wisdom to a young agent on the nature of people.

"'And this Agent Nichol, is the key. It's choice.'

'Choice?'

'We choose our thoughts. We choose our perceptions. We choose our attitudes. We may not think so. We may not believe it, but we do. I absolutely know we do. I've seen enough evidence, time after time, tragedy after tragedy. Triumph after triumph. It's about choice.'"

As book four of the Psalms closes we are being challenged to consider our choices. How will we look to the past? How will we envision the future? Will we lean towards trusting in God's provision or fearing that God will not be traveling with us into tomorrow?

---

[2] Penny, Louise. *Still Life: (Chief Inspector Gamache Novel Book 1)*, St. Martin's Minotaur, 2005, 80.

I feel it's likely I will do both. I'll do better at it sometimes than I will at others. What's important is cultivating a place in my spiritual being that is able to celebrate God's presence on the journey and work at making the choice of trusting that for the future even when – especially when – that future appears fraught with challenges.

Prayer

Faithful God, help me today and every day to choose to look back in awe at your mighty acts and into the future with anticipation and hope. Amen.

Day 38

Psalms 107, 108

Psalm 107 is about the faithful finding multiple ways to get lost. It's subjects are not those who have never known or have always rejected God. It's about those who once were found, but now are lost.

"Some of the redeemed had wandered
  into the desert, into the wasteland,
  they couldn't find their way
  to a city or town." (107:4)

"Some of the redeemed had been sitting
  in darkness and deep gloom;
        they were prisoners suffering in chains...." (107:10)

"Some of the redeemed were fools
  because of their sinful ways.
  they suffered because of
  their wickedness." (107:17)

"Some of the redeemed had gone out
  on the ocean in ships,
  making their living on the high seas." (107:23)

Some wander into the desert, while others go out on to the ocean in ships. However they go, they go away from the will and the provision of God, not realizing what is happening till a moment of desperation leads them to recognize their plight and cry out to God. In each instance God has not left anyone - instead folks have wittingly or not chosen to leave God.

I have wandered into the desert a few times. I have felt the pull of the ships heading out to the ocean. I have, in short, been foolish. The thanksgiving here is that when I call out to God, God has a history of hearing me and helping me to find my way back.

Prayer

Forgiving God, I cannot stray so far that you will not be with me. When I feel lost help me to find the voice to call to you and trust that you will lead me home. Amen.

Day 39

Psalms 109, 110, 111, 112

Today's readings contain themes of youthful creative vitality, the consequences of decisions made for good or ill, taking the long view on what is of value and for what we will work in this life (transitory wealth and power vs. a solid reputation for righteousness that will endure) and our interaction with God all along the way.

Over the years I've heard many older Christians describe a transition that takes place in their lives. In my mid-fifties their words ring increasingly true in my experience.

The transition is from concern for things, material possessions, the trappings of success, to a contentedness with whatever is on hand and a much greater valuation on relationships and experiences.

Accumulation of stuff ultimately, live long enough, leads to a releasing of stuff and a desire for less. Grandparents aren't excited about their new gadget, they are endlessly excited about their grandchildren.

We grow older and our vision turns from what we will accomplish to how we will be remembered.

These Psalms guide us to the insight that the way we will be remembered is from how we have lived our lives. The most life-giving path is to as much as possible from our earliest days follow after the heart of God.

We will not always get it right, but our best path in youth, middle age and in our later years is to always aim to keep God's praise and God's call ever before us.

Prayer

Guide me to reflect on your righteousness and, with your direction and support, to aim for righteous choices, purposes and deeds. Amen.

Day 40

Psalms 113, 114, 115, 116

Where is heaven? Up in the sky? Beyond the clouds? We have telescopes that allow us to see well beyond what the biblical writers would have dreamed, but I don't believe we've yet photographed a "Welcome To Heaven" sign as our technology has rocketed through space.

Psalm 113 gives some help in showing how limited our language and really our thinking is when it comes to heaven.

"Who could possibly
    compare to the Lord our God?
 God rules from on high;
    he has to come down
    to even see heaven and earth!" (113:5-6)

Earth we know because we make our life here. Heaven we hope for and we have ideas perhaps of what we want it to be like. Somewhere beyond all that we can conceptualize and articulate is God. The psalmist here uses words to point out the limitations of words. God rules from on high - a place from which God has to "come down" to see heaven and earth.

Discussions of what heaven will be like are not unusual in Sunday School and Bible studies. It's understandable to have a curiosity about the nature of what our beliefs point to as the next step beyond this life. Often the heaven we imagine is a place that is the best of what we can imagine from our present experience. My standard answer in these conversations is that I don't know what heaven will be like, I just know that I want to be there. So I might imagine that it must be a place of friends and family, coffee and comic books, baseball and soccer, Skyline Chili and Imo's Pizza, but...I just don't know.

Psalm 113 invites us to picture an expanse of heaven and earth, the extremes we hold in our understanding and then know that God is bigger and somehow still beyond whatever boundaries we might imagine.

Prayer

We give thanks for the joys and challenges of this life - for the gift that this life is. We look forward with joyful anticipation to the future you hold for us. Amen.

Week Nine
Psalms 117-132

Day 41
Psalms 117, 118

Day 42
Psalm 119:1-88

Day 43
Psalm 119:89-176

Day 44
Psalms 120, 121, 122, 123, 124, 125, 126

Day 45
Psalms 127, 128, 129, 130, 131, 132

"I rejoice with those who said to me,
'Let's go to the Lord's house!'
Now our feet are standing
in your gates, Jerusalem!"
-Psalm 122:1-2

Day 41

Psalms 117, 118

It is a joy to have the opportunity to board an airplane and travel to a faraway place. I really do not complain about air travel much because it is such a miracle and it is such a privilege to be able to do it. I will say that when you are boarding for a flight of ten to twelve hours and you are walking back to your seat in the normal part of the plane there is a twinge of wistful jealousy when you walk through what appears to be the roomy accommodations of first class.

I recall one flight from New York to Tel Aviv. It was somewhere in the middle of the flight. The windows were closed and most of the lights were out to encourage us to sleep and many were giving it their best effort. I was in the center section, awake, wanting very much to go and walk up and down the aisle, but also not wanting to wake up the folks to either side of me (I was in the middle of the middle section).

To my right in one of the side sections I watched transfixed as a young woman stood and was apparently also wanting out. She was next to the window and the two people between her and the aisle were both out cold. And then it happened.

Looking very much like Spider-man, she climbed up in her seat and using the arms and tops of surrounding chairs she crawled out and gracefully, dropping herself lightly into the walkway. Most folks missed it, but the few of us who saw what happened wanted very much to stand and applaud her effort. Perhaps more impressive, she returned to her seat the same way she came out.

Life can feel like being stuck in a seat in an airplane, hemmed in by sleeping fellow travelers and no way to get to the aisle and freedom. The psalmist calls that "tight circumstances" and writes that,

> "In tight circumstances,
> I cried out to the Lord.
> The Lord answered me
> With wide-open spaces." (118:5)

Sometimes what we most need is a bit of room to breathe. It can be easy to feel overwhelmed by demands and deadlines, real and imagined, and the pressure we sometimes feel not to let anyone down. We on occasion even take pride in how busy we are as it affirms that we are needed - right up until it is too much. The psalmist identifies one of the greatest gifts God can grant us - a new perspective, a better pace, and a nice, long aisle on a full airplane.

Prayer

Holy God, as you hear us cry out from tight circumstances, deliver us to wide-open spaces. Amen.

"The Lord answered me with wide-open spaces."

Day 42

Psalm 119:1-88

How many ways can you name law? Instruction. Statutes. Rules. Precepts. Commandments. Each of these comes up multiple times in the first half of Psalm 119. There is talk of the paths we travel on, the proper turning of our hearts, keeping commandments, living by God's righteousness and more.

It's a wonderful long slow walk that praises God for the guidelines that God has shared with us, while in its very repetition acknowledging that keeping these laws and staying on this righteous path is a great challenge.

We face challenges from external forces that would pull us from God's path. And, truth be told, we face challenges from within, when we see a path we imagine to be more to our liking or more advantageous to us.

This is a long meditation on the value of immersing ourselves in the study of God's instruction. Such study guides us towards a better understanding of the God we aim to serve:

"Now teach me your statutes!

Help me understand

what your precepts are about

so I can contemplate

your wondrous works." (119:26-27)

With study and understanding we move towards the joy of living in alignment with God's will:

"I will walk around in wide-open spaces,

because I have pursued your precepts.

...I will rejoice in your commandments

because I love them.

I will lift up my hands

to your commandments

because I love them,

and I will contemplate all your statutes." (119:45, 46-47)

God's laws are there not to frustrate us and not to set impossible standards of which we are bound to fall short. God's laws are a gift to guide us towards the best possible life, one spent seeking after the heart of God.

Prayer

Thank you for your guidance. Give me a heart that longs to learn your way so that I may walk in your paths and rejoice in your presence. Amen.

Day 43

Psalm 119:89-176

After one hundred seventy-six verses and twenty-two poems - one for each letter of the Hebrew alphabet...after many, many reflections on the law and the wonder of this gift from God...once we've completed the concerns about that which would pull the psalmist off track and the pledges to continue to study and revere God's instruction, this is where we are left at the end:

"I've wandered off like a sheep, lost.

Find your servant

because I haven't forgotten

your commandments." (119:176)

The sheer length of the Psalm points to a core truth of its content. Faith is both a glorious truth and an often difficult, long and uphill slog. "A long obedience in the same direction" are words originally belonging to Friedrich Nietzsche, more recently employed in a Christian context by pastor Eugene Peterson.[1] Peterson wrote a book with that title and those words come to me regularly when I reflect on the life of following Jesus.

---

[1] Peterson, Eugene. *A Long Obedience In The Same Direction: Discipleship In An Instant Society,* InterVarsity Press, 1980.

This is not a sprint. It's not about one great moment and the rest not mattering. It is about that journey that is both beautiful and hard, sublime and fraught with despair.

We marvel at the sunrise and then tremble at the morning news. We see acts of kindness, generosity and compassion and without shifting our gaze see injustice, indifference and disregard for the well-being of others. To paraphrase the apostle Paul I look at my own actions and am saddened by how regularly they do not match up with my aspirations as to who I want to be as a person of faith.

Psalm 119 gets that. It doesn't build to a crescendo. It builds to something along the lines of...the journey continues. However long a lifetime is, faith is a work of a lifetime. Step by step, grace by grace, guided by God towards a long obedience in the same direction.

Prayer

Keep our eyes on you. Keep us hungry for your instruction. Keep us mindful of our inability to do this on our own. Amen.

Day 44

Psalms

120, 121, 122, 123, 124, 125, 126

Today's readings are the first seven of the fifteen Psalms of Ascent. The translation I typically use - the Common English Bible - labels them as pilgrimage songs. Both are accurate descriptions, but the idea of ascent captures an additional element that is key to visualizing the journey of the pilgrims. Jerusalem is literally a city on a hill, several hills actually, and the temple sits atop Mount Zion.

If a pilgrim is coming from the north to Jerusalem they typically would travel along the Jordan River and then come from Jericho, near the Dead Sea, the lowest place on the earth up to Jerusalem. It's a very real ascent. Even in the vicinity of the Temple itself one might find oneself on the Mount of Olives, crossing the Kidron Valley and, again, climbing up, up, up to the Temple.

The impossible to know for certain speculation by scholars is that this group of Psalms was utilized particularly by pilgrims on their approach to the Temple.

It's a wonderful image to think of the combination of the spiritual and physical ascent taking place as one climbed the holy hill and eventually the stairs leading up to the area surrounding the Temple proper.

The language speaks of journeying towards that higher place with expectation:

"I raise my eyes towards the mountains.

 Where will my help come from?

 My help comes from the Lord,

 the maker of heaven and earth." (121:1-2)

It was, of course, no accident that cities were placed on hills. Not only did it allow the Temple to be elevated in a strong bit of spiritual symbolism, but it also allowed the very practical benefit of being able to look out from a high vantage point and see who might be coming towards the city. It was a safety precaution.

"Mountains surround Jerusalem.

 That's how the Lord

 surrounds his people

 from now until forever from now!" (125:2)

One of my favorite passages from the Psalms can be found in Psalm 22 which is something of a love letter to Jerusalem. It begins with the joy of arrival:

"I rejoice with those who said to me,

 'Let's go to the Lord's house!'

No our feet are standing

In your gates, Jerusalem!" (122:1-2)

This joy is accompanied by a desire to keep the holy city secure. It is possible that these Psalms were written after the exile to Babylon. If so one could imagine the sense of wanting very much to hold on to what had once been lost and had now been restored to the people in terms of Jerusalem in general and the Temple itself.

"Pray that Jerusalem has peace;

'Let those who love you have rest.

Let there be peace on your walls;

Let there be rest on your fortifications.'

For the sake of my family and friends,

I say, 'Peace be with you, Jerusalem.'" (122:6-8)

At a popular pilgrimage site today known as the Garden Tomb, there is an ancient tomb surrounded by a lovely well maintained garden. It's a beautiful place to pray and worship. As you walk through the garden there are small signs quoting scripture placed here and there on the path. One of them, nestled in amongst the greenery and flowers says, "Pray For The Peace Of Jerusalem." It is a reminder that the inner desire for a place of peace is as real now as it was when the Psalmist said very much the same thing out of the same yearning. And it is also a reminder of how very challenging finding that peace can be.

Prayer

Bring peace to Jerusalem, to each one of us, and to our world. Help us to work towards that for which we ask. Amen.

The Garden Tomb, Jerusalem

Day 45

Psalms

127, 128, 129, 130, 131, 132

There is not a wasted moment in Psalm 132. From the depths of verse 1 to the affirmation of God's redemption in verse 8, every word is carefully chosen and rings true in our human experience. I remember very long nights when I was growing up. Nights when I did not feel well, typically with nothing more troubling than a fever and an upset stomach, but which in my young mind seemed life threatening. As bad as how I felt physically at any one moment, was how long it seemed to go on. I would lie in bed and sleep fitfully. When I woke up I would think, surely it is daylight now, but it was still night and it seemed to go on and on and on.

Just a few years ago now, my mother-in-law was battling cancer and some nights I would stay in the hospital room with her. Some nights it felt exactly like those nights from my boyhood. She might get restless, be uncomfortable, need a drink of water or simply be disoriented in the wee small hours of the morning. The nurse might come in with medication. In those moments it could seem like the time from midnight till 6:00 a.m. lasted about fourteen hours.

Morning always comes.

When we find ourselves in the depths - sometimes simply because of circumstances, sometimes because of our own actions (this is a penitential Psalm) - a beautiful truth about faith is that God never leaves. We trust that before we see it. We sit in darkness and with our whole being keep our eyes fixed on the horizon where the sun will rise.

"My whole being waits for my Lord -
  more than the night watch
  waits for the morning;
  yes, more than the night watch
  waits for the morning!
 Israel, wait for the Lord!
 Because faithful love is with the Lord;
  because great redemption
  is with our God!" (130:6-7)

Prayer

When it is night, when the depths feel truly deep, keep me focused on the morning that will surely come. Amen.

Week Ten

Psalms 133-150

Day 46
Psalms 133, 134, 135, 136

Day 47
Psalms 137, 138, 139, 140

Day 48
Psalms 141, 142, 143, 144

Day 49
Psalms 145, 146

Day 50
Psalms 147, 148, 149, 150

"Teach me to do what pleases you,
because you are my God.
Guide me by your good spirit
into a good land."
-Psalm 143:10

Day 46

Psalms 133, 134, 135, 136

A team wins a championship in sports. The players are celebrating, they put on their championship hats and t-shirts and walk around smiling and hugging one another. Reporters begin speaking to them about how it feels to win. They have worked and worked. Usually for an entire regular season, through some sort of play-off and finally winning a championship game or series. It should be a moment of elation and it kind of is, but usually one of those questions very quickly takes a bit of the shine off things: Do you think you'll be able to repeat?

Life can make it hard to celebrate arriving.

You don't have to be a sports team to work hard to arrive at a destination. It can be anything that we have had to exert effort on in the journey to reach a set point along the way. I don't know if Psalm 135 was intentionally placed as the first Psalm after the Psalms of Ascent, but it feels perfect. It is praise from beginning to end and it is set as an offering of praise from within God's Temple.

Praise the Lord!
　　Praise the Lord's name!
　　All you who serve the Lord, praise God!
All you who stand in the Lord's house—
　　　who stand in the courtyards of our God's
　　　temple—
　　praise the Lord, because the Lord is good!
　　　Sing praises to God's name because it is
　　　beautiful! (135:1-3)

It can be challenging to allow a moment of complete celebration. To have a moment of simply being about praise. Even as we place ourselves in God's presence in prayer, in worship, or in a time of fellowship, the joy can be fleeting because life intrudes. The concerns we brought with us don't want to be quiet. The anxiety we have been feeling will not subside. Our to-do list behaves like pop-up ads on a computer website, distracting our attention from where we mean for it to be.

Here is the psalmist modeling a moment of exulting in having made the ascent and rejoicing in God's presence. When we reach a moment of prayer and praise, when we stand for a moment at a time of destination, it is a time of rejoicing. The journey and the work will be there waiting when we pick up our packs and are ready to begin again. Don't overlook or race past the celebration.

Prayer

Grant us the wisdom to not only work on the journey, but to celebrate the arrivals. Amen.

Day 47

Psalms 137, 138, 139, 140

Author and pastor Brian McLaren[1] offers a helpful insight to the way we grow into the Bible. "As we progress through the biblical library, stories interact with one another again and again. Together they reveal an ever fuller and deeper vision of God." McLaren's point is one that resonates very specifically with me as I think about this journey through the Psalms and my intention to go back to the beginning again and continue to make my way through for the foreseeable future. They feed off of one another.

The language of the Psalms creates a rich lexicon for speaking of God and for speaking with God.

Psalm 139 would be impressive on its own. It's a beautiful poem about the intimate way God knows us. The scope of God's creativity and vision is beyond our capacity to take in and yet God knows us in every detail.

---

[1] McLaren, Brian. *Seeking Aliveness: Daily Reflections On A New Way To Experience and Practice the Christian Faith*, FaithWords, Hachette Book Group, 2017, 37.

Coming where it does in the Psalter however, having read 138 Psalms before arriving at this one, we have considered many of these thoughts before.

How vast and how holy is our God. What a miraculous gift it is to be here and experience the beauty of God's creation. God's availability to hear our prayers when we are crying out in anguish and when we are rejoicing. It's all come up, most of it multiple times.

As we encounter it all again in Psalm 139 there is a familiarity and at the same time a uniqueness to it that is especially beautiful when it is considered and heard as part of the larger body of work.

It is like a baseball game in September. In a normal year each team plays 162 games. Each game follows rules that in most instances have been around for many years. We know what a baseball game looks like. And yet there is always the possibility of something being done in a particular game that was never done before.

My Cincinnati Reds recently, in a rare post-season appearance over these past few years played a game that featured more strikeouts by both teams combined than any other game in post-season history. The game was finally won by Atlanta in the 13th inning, but it was the first time in post-season history that a game had gone 0-0 through 12 innings.

We are deep into the Psalms, the conclusion is in sight, and then this bit of brilliance emerges speaking of now familiar considerations in these striking words:

"Lord, you have examined me.

You know me.

You know when I sit down

and when I stand up.

Even from far away,

you comprehend my plans.

You study my traveling and resting.

You are thoroughly familiar

with all my ways." (Psalm 139:1-3)

I give thanks today for Psalm 139 and for its 149 companions that create a wonderful collection of invitations to contemplate in ever increasing depth, our Creator.

Prayer

Holy God, you have searched me, examined me - you know me. Thank you for loving me still and inviting me to know and love you. Amen.

Day 48

Psalms 141, 142, 143, 144

"Teach me to do what pleases you,

   because you are my God.

  Guide me by your good spirit

   into a good land." (143:10)

"This is a very simple game. You throw the ball, you catch the ball, you hit the ball." With these words Nuke LaLoosh, in the film *Bull Durham*, summarized the basic mechanics of baseball. Under the tutelage of veteran catcher Crash Davis, Nuke learned not to complicate when simplicity would suffice. Sure, baseball is a million variables and situations that a lover of the game can go on about for days (I speak from personal experience), but what are the necessities? Throw. Catch. Hit.

Sometimes in life we find our way to that kind of awareness. This brand of clarity shows up in Psalm 143:10. It's ultimately about fundamental motivation. The heart of the desire to be faithful is born of a desire to be who God has created us to be. The purist stirrings of our heart towards praise arise because of who we are and who God is and occasional glimpses of the truth of what that relationship looks like.

Do we want to arrive at a good land? Most days, yes. So many people, things, programs want to present themselves as the guide that can get us there. There is likely benefit in a lot of it. But it's all about God's guidance, because it's God's good land and God is the source of any and all truly effective help in moving in that direction.

"Teach me to do what pleases you." The psalmist might paraphrase Nuke - it's a very simple faith. Not easy and not without a million variables and situations, but a heart that wants to be shaped by it's maker is an irreplaceable beginning point.

Prayer

Teach me to do what pleases you. Guide me by your good Spirit. Amen.

Day 49

Psalms 145, 146

When running a set distance I usually break the race up into three parts. The first third I try to run hard, but not so hard that I'm overextended. The second part I dial back a bit, try to hold my place and stay focused. The third part of the goal is to finish well. My hope is that nothing much will be left in the tank so that when the finish line is in sight I can go all out and try not to feel like I held something back from a full effort.

With Psalm 145, the finish line is in sight. This Psalm sets the tone that will see the collection through to its completion. Praise. Full on praise to close strong and finish on a high note. Of the final five Psalms, 145 is the only one that doesn't begin with the words "Praise the Lord".

As I read this poem, the last of the Psalms attributed to David, I was outside on an early fall morning, on a deck overlooking a lake in the North Carolina portion of the Great Smoky Mountains. It could not have been a more fitting setting for inspiring praise.

The lake was right there in plain view, then within thirty minutes covered completely in fog that rolled in as I read. Eventually the view cleared, the lake reappeared and the colors shifted constantly as the sun climbed above the mountains.

"I will lift you up high, my God,
the true king.
I will bless your name forever and always.
The Lord is great
and so worthy of praise!" (145:1-2)

I was reminded of these words written by pastor Lillian Daniel: "Anyone can find God alone on a picturesque mountaintop. The miracle is that we can find God in the company of other people as annoying as we are."[2] Similarly, on a sparkling fall morning it was easy to resonate with the psalmist's exuberant praise. The miracle is that we can praise God wherever we are, in whatever circumstance and alongside of folks just as fallible as us.

Wherever you find yourself this day, with whomever you are sharing the journey, whatever the challenges before you, take a moment to proclaim the Lord's praise.

---

[2] Daniel, Lillian. *Tired of Apologizing for a Church I Don't Belong To: Spirituality without Stereotypes, Religion without Ranting*, FaithWords, 2016, 22.

Prayer

I will bless your name today and every day. Hold me to this promise. Help me to offer praise today, tomorrow and each day of my life. Amen.

Lake Junaluska, North Carolina

Day 50

Psalms 147, 148, 149, 150

The Hebrew title of the book of Psalms is Tehillim which means "Praises". Clearly as we've read through the compete Psalter there have been a wide variety of poems, not all of them psalms of praise. Praise, though, is the title of the collection and perhaps can be understood then as the ultimate goal of the editors who assembled the book.

After everything, after the laments, after the expressions of abandonment, after the fear of enemies and forces of nature, after and beyond it all, there is God and there is praise. Psalm 150 is a glorious final word.

Beginning with God in God's sanctuary, a band of musicians is called to offer praise. The focus is on volume. A blast of the ram's horn. Drums. Loud cymbals. Clashing cymbals. This is no delicate, introspective composition, this is raucous and joyful and will almost certainly lead to dancing.

The scope is all encompassing. It's beyond a call to the people of Jerusalem, or the citizens of Israel. It is an invitation to every last thing drawing breath to use that breath to praise God (literally Hallelujah). It is a great capstone on a remarkably diverse group of expressions of what it means to relate to God. There has been no glossing over the rough spots in life in the Psalms. These songs and poems have looked unflinchingly at how faithfulness can be a struggle and how we can be as capable of despair as of joy.

Praise gets the last word. There is great hope here for the life of faith. If you've hurt, if you've been angry, if you've felt lost, you haven't been doing anything wrong – it's all a part of the journey for most people. Our trust though is that behind it all there is hope. For today and for all the days. Forever. When you are struggling remember to blow the rams horn. When you cannot take one more setback, clash the cymbals. Through it all join your voice with every living thing. Praise the Lord!

Hallelujah!

Prayer

This day I offer praise for who you are, what you have done, what you are doing and for what the future holds. Hallelujah. Amen.

Final Words

Thank you for joining me on this journey through the book of Psalms. Further projects are in the works, including a "With A Friend" devotional for the book of Acts as well as a "Through The Bible In A Year With A Friend." There is also an Advent Devotional based on travel experiences in the Holy Land and a Devotional History Of The Pandemic composed of daily meditations over one hundred days early in the COVID-19 pandemic.

I enjoy engaging with scripture and sharing that journey with you. If you would like to share your thoughts and reactions with me, or be notified as these further projects reach completion, please contact me at hebronpcusa@gmail.com.

Celebrate Life!

George

Made in the USA
Monee, IL
20 April 2022